For Deniz

© Copyright 2014

Written by Sally A Jones and Amanda C Jones
Illustrations by Annalisa C Jones

Published by GUINEA PIG EDUCATION

2 Cobs Way,
New Haw,
Addlestone,
Surrey,
KT15 3AF.
www.guineapigeducation.co.uk

NO part of this publication may be reproduced, stored or copied for commercial purposes and profit without the prior written permission of the publishers.

ISBN: 978-1-907733-83-3

Dear Kids and Parents,

This book contains a structured course to teach children to spell using phonics.

A friendly character, an alien called Zoggy, takes your child on a journey: he introduces them to word building, focusing on areas that cause spelling difficulty; including long vowel sounds, 'ea' sounds, soft 'c' and soft 'g', and silent letters.

Each challenge includes funny phonic rhymes, phrases and sentences to reinforce the sounds being taught; learn them off by heart, practise rewriting them from memory. There are also a series of exercises to help your child practise spelling, including tests where your child can read, copy, cover and spell.

MEET Zoggy...

ZOGGY has been sent from planet ZEN, three million light years away.

ZOGGY'S FIRST CHALLENGE

IS THERE ANYBODY OUT THERE?
IS THERE ANYTHING, ANYBODY
OR ANYONE OUT THERE?

I WANT TO MEET THE ALIENS OF EARTH.

I WANT EVERYONE, EVERYBODY, EVERYTHING TO COME AND GET SOME SPELLING HELP FROM ZOGGY.

READ	COPY	COVER & SPELL
ever		
never		
every		
everything		
everybody		
everyone		
everywhere		
any		
many		
anyone		
anybody		
anything		
anywhere		

Can you write seven words from ever?

1. ....
2. ....
3. ....
4. ....
5. ....
6. ....
7. ....

... And six words from any?

1. ....
2. ....
3. ....
4. ....
5. ....
6. ....

ZOGGY'S SECOND CHALLENGE

HAIL RAIN

What do I think about the good old British weather?

Cover and write:

DON'T COMPLAIN ABOUT THE RAIN AGAIN.

GET TRAINING. IT'S ALWAYS RAINING.

ZOGGY REPORTS BACK...

IT IS COLD AND WET HERE. WHAT A PAIN. I FEEL DRAINED. MY TRAINERS ARE RUINED. THE RAIN IS DRIPPING DOWN MY BACK AND I FEEL A NEW SENSATION... I'M SHAKING... IT'S CALLED SHIVERING...

READ	COPY	COVER & SPELL
rain		
raining		
brain		
Britain		
complain		
hail stone		
again		
drain		
trainers		
restrain		
refrain		
training		

ZOGGY'S THIRD CHALLENGE

DO I LIKE TO BE BESIDE THE SEASIDE?

Zoggy:

What do I see BEFORE me?

What do I see BEHIND me?

What do I see BETWEEN me and...?

READ	COPY	COVER & SPELL
before		
behind		
between		

Zoggy says,

" **Can you say 'ay' as in make?**

Can you say 'ee' as in these?

Can you say 'o' as in the water is freezing on my toe?

Can you say 'i' as in sand pie?

Can you say 'ue' as in the sea is blue? "

THEN YOU KNOW YOUR LONG VOWEL SOUNDS.

Look at these words:

Do I see a shark **FIN** out there in the sea?
No, it's **FINE**. It is only a dolphin.

If we add an 'e', 'a magic e', it jumps back two letters and makes the 'i' long.

Can you find some _long vowel sounds_ in Zoggy's poem?

Look at the pie I have **made,**
With my bucket and my **spade.**

Do I feel a strong sea **breeze**?
Sitting here, I think I'll **freeze.**

What shall I do at high **tide**?
Should I have a donkey **ride**?

Watch the band, the big **trombone,**
Play about on my smart **phone.**

Ride the great big surfing **waves.**
Is it my warm towel that I **crave**?

The water's cold, I'm turning **blue,**
My teeth are chattering and that is **true.**

The weather on earth is **extreme;**
It all amounts to a bad **dream.**

MESSAGE TO PLANET ZEN...

YOU WON'T BELIEVE THIS! EARTHLINGS LIKE TO
SIT ON   HARD STONES ON THE BEACH IN THEIR
UNDERWEAR. THEY WEAR SHADES OVER THEIR EYES.
IT'S CALLED SUN BATHING BUT THERE IS NO SUN.
IT'S CRAZY HERE.

I'VE COLLECTED SOME SPECIMENS TO BRING HOME:

- DARK SHADES FOR THE EYES
- TUBE OF STICKY STUFF TO RUB ON THE BODY
- SHOES THAT DON'T COVER THE FEET
- A WARM STRIPY CLOTH

Can you guess what he collected?

READ	COPY	COVER & SPELL
made		
spade		
feel		
breeze		
freeze		
extreme		
tide		
ride		
home		
mobile phone		
these		
toe		
computer		
trombone		
before		
behind		
between		
beside		
true		
blue		
supreme		

ZOGGY'S FOURTH CHALLENGE

It's half past two in the afternoon and it is still raining. Zoggy watches the rain drip down the windowpane of his spacecraft.

Pick out a word with the same sounds for each box from these phrases.

It is still rainy,
It is quite stormy.

It is making me shiver,
It is making me quiver.

My hair has gone curly,
My bodywork is dirty.

I am feeling such dismay,
I cannot go out and play.

But let's not be gloomy
Let's go and **party**!

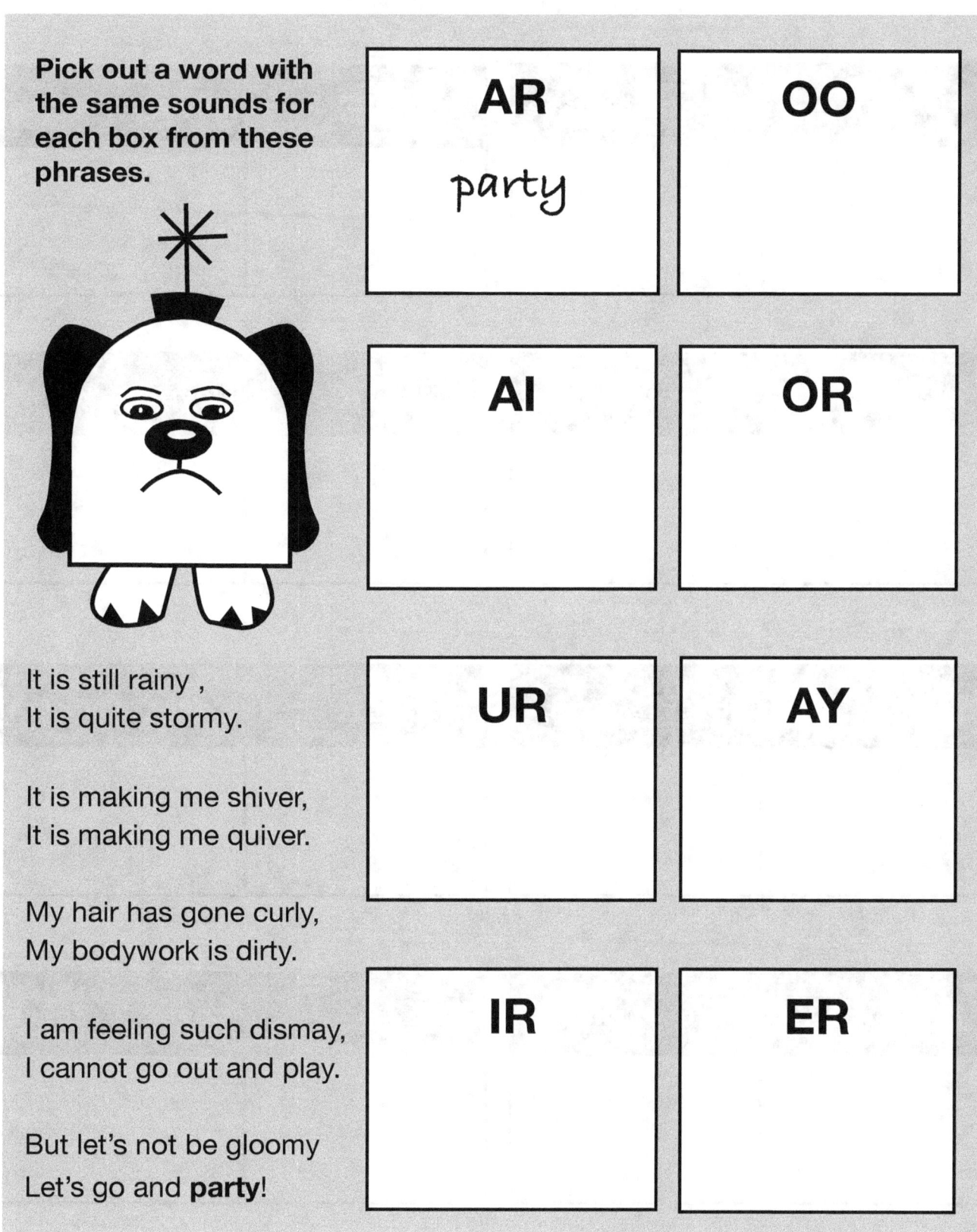

AR — party

OO

AI

OR

UR

AY

IR

ER

Put the words below in the right boxes?

freeze	rainy	gloomy	smart
stormy	party	dirty	quiver
shiver	breeze	asked	dismay
curly	past	sport	afternoon

OO	Cover & Write

EE	Cover & Write

AR	Cover & Write

OR	Cover & Write

UR, IR	Cover & Write

ER	Cover & Write

AI, AY	Cover & Write

AS (AS IN ASK)	Cover & Write

ZOGGY'S FIFTH CHALLENGE

"What's next Zoggy?"

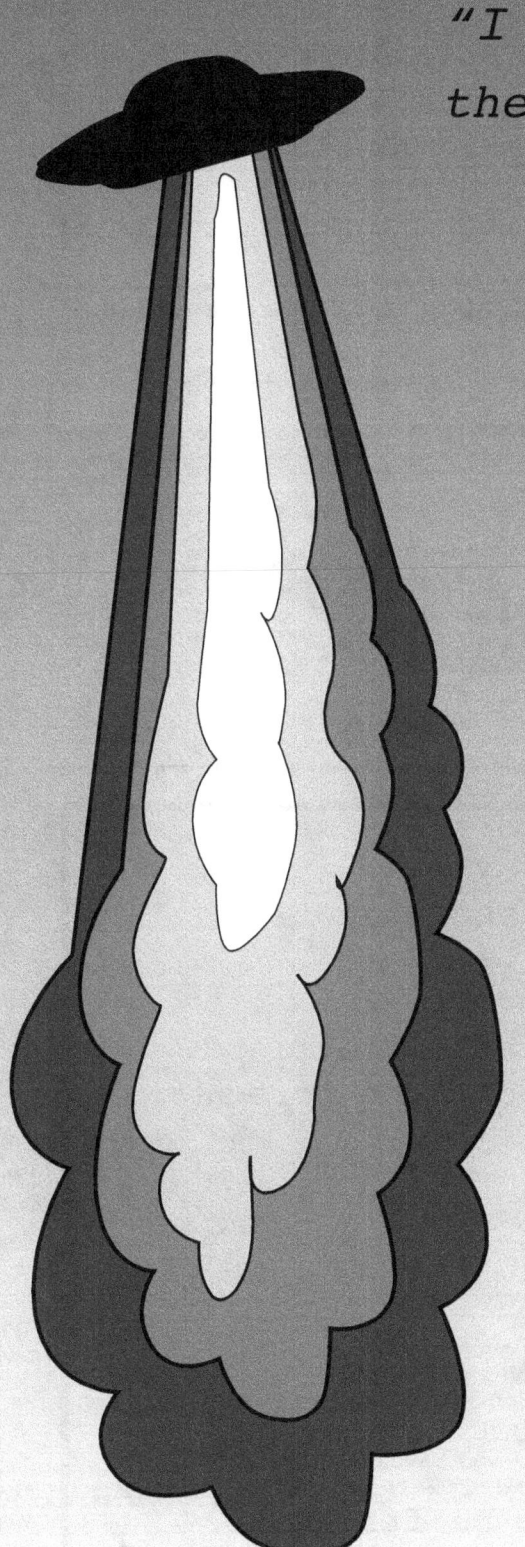

"I think I will EXPLORE the airways over earth."

PREPARE FOR TAKE OFF!

5
4
3
2
1

ZOOM!

REPORT BACK TO ZEN...

BECAUSE IT'S **ALREADY** DAY 2 OF MY VISIT TO EARTH, THE NEXT THING I MUST DO IS TO EXPLORE THE AIRWAYS.

ALTHOUGH IT'S EARLY IN THE DAY, THE FLIGHT PATHS OVER BRITAIN ARE **ALMOST** FULL. THEY'RE NOT VERY TECHNOLOGICALLY ADVANCED HERE. THE PEOPLE OF EARTH **ALWAYS** FLY **ALTOGETHER** IN CONTRAPTIONS CALLED PLANES!

It's useful to remember that X is NEVER, NEVER, followed by S.

Up here I'm learning how to use my intergalactic Z.A.T NAV to scan the planet Earth. Whoops... Wrong button...!

I'm coming into land my space craft in a field. I have more exploring to do. I won't be bored.

<u>What can I see?</u>

- a house
- a horse... of course...
- three young humans are approaching me...

.... but they have turned out to be friendly. What a relief!

READ	COPY	COVER & SPELL
because		
house		
horse		
course		
although		
already		
almost		
always		
altogether		
explore		
more		
bored		
learning		
learn		
earth		
early		
search		
field		
friends		
relief		

ZOGGY'S SIXTH CHALLENGE

'<u>EA</u>' is the *Master* of *Disguise*

"Let's go Zoggy," say the kids, "Are you *ready*? Are you *steady*? Do you like our dreadful weather?"

---

1. **Yes, number 1 is the 'ea' sound in <u>ready.</u>**

2. **Yes, number 2 is the 'ea' sound in <u>ear</u> or <u>appear</u>.**

   Can you hear with your ear? Do you fear what might appear?

3. **Yes, number 3 is 'ea' as in <u>treat</u>.**

   What do you eat? Would meat be a treat?

4. **You've got it number 4 is 'ea' as in <u>heart</u>.**

   Does your heart beat faster when you face a disaster?

5. **Yes, number 5 is 'ea' as in <u>wear</u>.**

   What do you wear? Try some human kids gear.

6. **Yes, number 6 is 'ea' as in <u>break</u>.**

   Isn't it great to have a break on planet earth?

'I' before 'E' except after 'C,'
but only when it sounds like ee.

REPORT BACK TO ZEN...

YOU ARE
YOUNGSTERS

ENCLOSE A VIEW OF MY FRIENDS I MET IN THE
FIELD. THESE ARE TYPICAL EXAMPLES OF HUMAN
KIDS. THEY HAVE A FOUR-LEGGED CREATURE WITH
THEM WHICH RUNS ROUND YAPPING.

READ	COPY	COVER & SPELL
friend		
friendly		
field		
relief		
view		
seaside		
creature		
beat		
heat		
read		
weather		
ready		
steady		
ear		
appear		
near		
nearly		
nearby		
year		
earth		
early		
search		
heard		
heart		
great		
break		

ZOGGY'S SEVENTH CHALLENGE

Zoggy visits a human house and says it's great to eat human food.

"<u>TWO</u> pieces of pie please."

Zoggy teaches you **soft c**. He says 'ce', 'ci', 'cy' are *soft sounds* like 's'. 'Ca' is a **hard sound**.

Dan, Sam and their sister Grace
invite Zoggy to their place.

The garden is big with lots of space,
Plenty of room to have a race.

Zoggy bounces on the trampoline,
jumping higher than you've ever seen.

They're really excited. That's for certain.
But whose that peeping through the curtain?

Mum, Collette, measures out rice.
She cooks a pie; it smells quite nice.

For pudding, they decide to eat ice cream.
A glass of juice; it's just a dream.

But Zoggy is full to capacity.
His metal frame has no elasticity.

The food is yummy,
But he's holding his tummy.

REPORT BACK TO ZEN...

EARTHLING FOOD SIMPLY IS DELICIOUS! IT IS MUCH BETTER THAN THE ZEN WORMS WE EAT ON OUR PLANET. I AM BRINGING BACK SOME EARTH RECIPES. BE SURE TO READ AND MEASURE THE INGREDIENTS CAREFULLY.

READ	COPY	COVER & SPELL
Grace		
rice		
place		
space		
race		
bounce		
bouncing		
excited		
excitement		
recipe		
certain		
city		
capacity		
elasticity		
medicine		
sure		
measure		
decide		
delicious		
precious		

Zoggy has eaten **two** pieces of pie. He ate **too** much **too** soon. **Does** Zoggy need a **dose** of medicine?

Zoggy says:

"Homophones are words that sound the same but have a different spelling and meaning."

Can you spell?

1. go, goes
2. do, does
3. lie, lies
4. lying
5. try, tries
6. trying

Write sentences using these tricky words...

1. to, too, two
2. write, right
3. where, were
4. peace, piece
5. does, dose
6. their, there, they're
7. threw, through

ZOGGY'S EIGHTH CHALLENGE

It's day three of Zoggy's visit.
The fair has come to <u>town</u>.

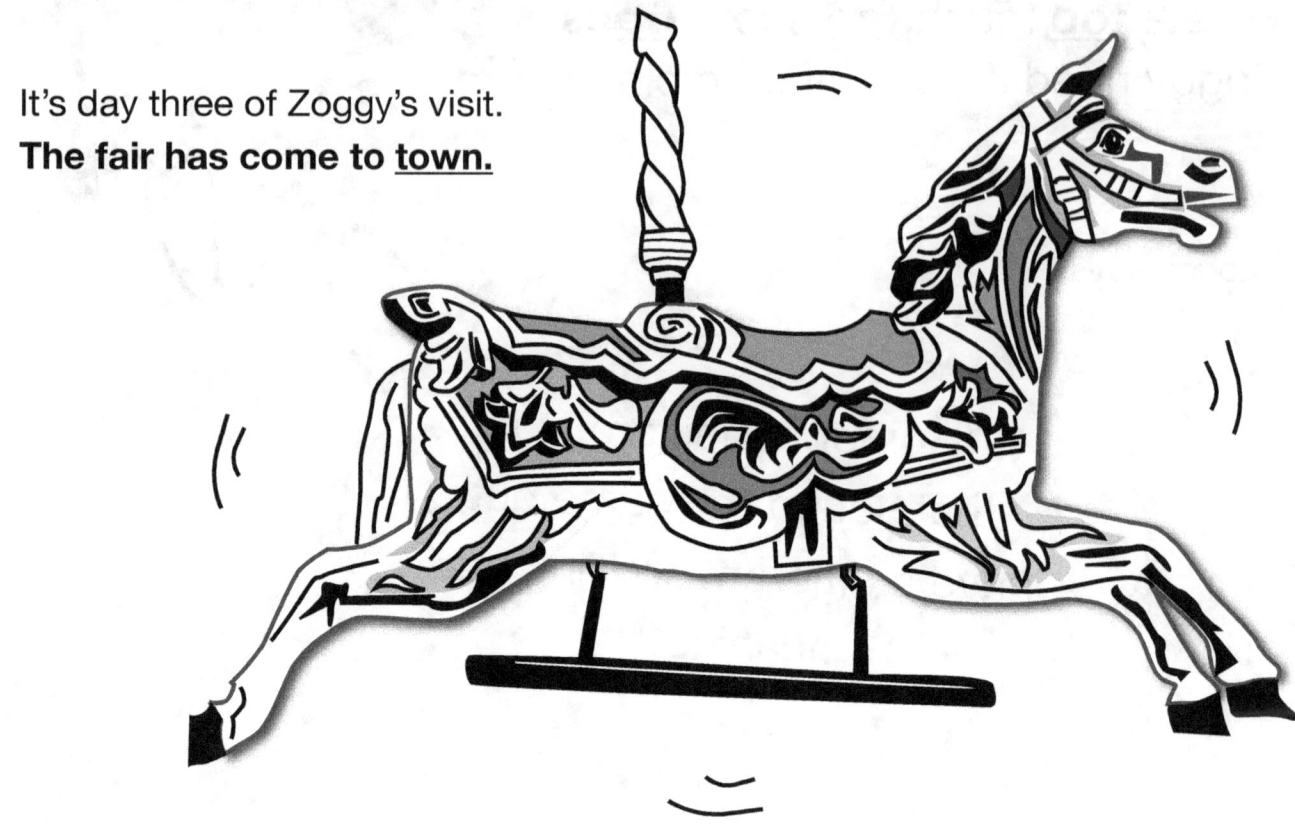

AIR	Where is the fair? It's over there.
GHT	It came at night by the first light.
EA	It's great! It's open late.
EA, EE	Let's get a treat, something sweet.
OU	WHIZZ round, above the ground.
EE	Ride the wheel. How does it feel?
ELL, EL	Ring the bell on the carousel.
CK	Hook up the duck, if you have the luck.
MAGIC E	Here the cries, I've won a prize.
AW	It's awesome. Yes!

REPORT BACK TO ZEN...

YESTERDAY I WOKE UP TO PANDEMONIUM. MY SPACECRAFT WAS SURROUNDED BY HOUSES ON WHEELS. I WAS MOANING. I WAS GROANING. I WAS TRAUMATISED, I CAN TELL YOU. THE HUMAN PEOPLE WERE WHIZZING THROUGH THE AIR ON MACHINES, YELLING AT THE TOP OF THEIR VOICES. MY HEAD WAS ACHING!

READ	COPY	COVER & SPELL
fair		
air		
where		
there		
their		
night		
light		
round		
surrounded		
ground		
shouting		
down town		
people		
pandemonium		
machine		
awesome		
moaning		
groaning		
noisy		

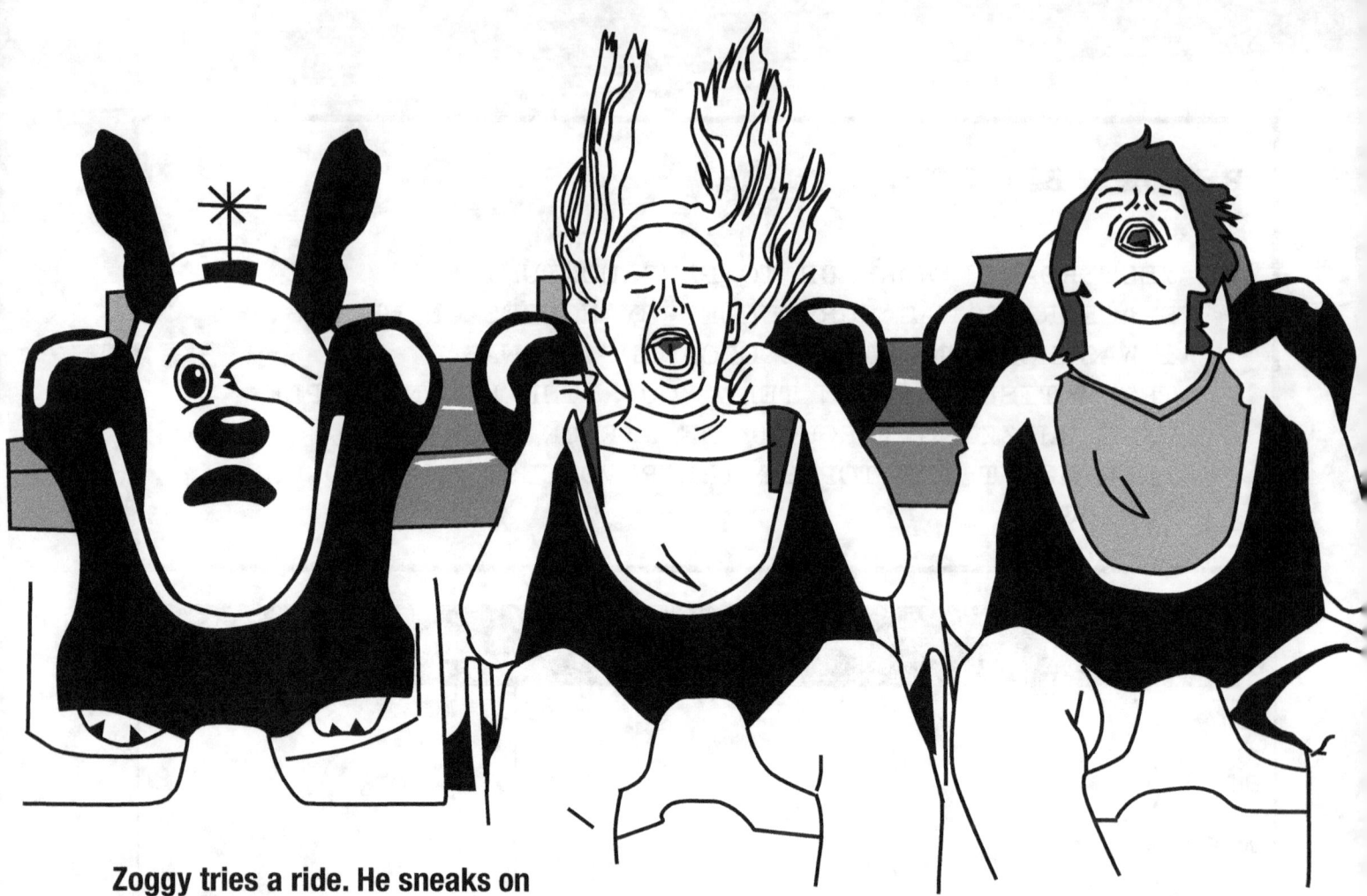

Zoggy tries a ride. He sneaks on when no one is looking. ENJOY!

What a noise!
Girls and boys,

Screaming and shouting,
The tension is mounting.

I want to have a go
My fear must not show.

I'm on the best ride in town:
It goes up, it goes down.

The feeling is ace,
Like hurtling through space.

I'm whizzing,
I'm dipping,

I'm fizzing,
I'm flipping.

The lights are glowing.
The ride is slowing.

Round and round,
We're back on the ground.
That was great!

Zoggy says:

"If a word has a short vowel sound, like 'a' in cat or 'i' in spin, you double the consonant to make most 'ing' words. (There are a few exceptions, like marketing)"

Double the consonant to make 'ing' words.

whiz   *whizzing*

dip   ....

fiz   ....

flip   ....

Zoggy says: "Find more words with these sounds."

OI NOISE	**OY** ENJOYMENT
OA GROAN	**DOUBLE LETTER** WHI ... ING
OW TOWN	**OU** SOUND
AU TRAUMA	**AW** AWESOME

Zoggy goes into the haunted house at the fair...

Can you answer these questions?

- **Who** has come to the crooked house?

- **What** were those STRANGE noises upstairs?

- **Whose** face is at the window?

Maybe you can put the **whole** story together. **Which** 'wh' word is the odd one out?

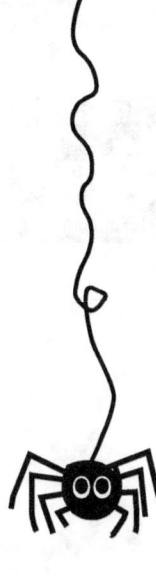

REPORT BACK TO ZEN...

HOW DID I DARE
GO TO THE FAIR?

I'VE HAD A BIG FRIGHT;
I'VE TURNED QUITE WHITE.

THE HALL OF MIRRORS
GAVE ME THE SHIVERS.

THE HAUNTED HOUSE
MADE ME CREEP LIKE A MOUSE.

I'M COMING AWAY
NO MONEY TO PAY.

....

YOU CAN FRIGHTEN YOURSELF WITH TALES OF SCARY
G... G... G... GHOSTS.

I'M BRINGING BACK SOME SPECIMENS — ROUND SHINY
METAL CIRCLES AND BITS OF PAPER THE EARTHLINGS
SWAP FOR THINGS. WHAT COULD THESE BE?

READ	COPY	COVER & SPELL
who		
what		
whose		
whole		
whom		
tail		
tales		
haunted		
ghost		
yourself		
myself		
fright		
frightened		
frightening		
strange		

Words with 'ge', 'gi', 'gy' often have a <u>soft sound</u>, as in 'giant'.

ZOGGY'S NINTH CHALLENGE

MATCH OF THE DAY

Write and remember the underlined words.

Are you **ROUGH** and **TOUGH** **ENOUGH** to play a **THOROUGHLY** **ROUGH** game of footie?

It was my **dream**
to join the **team.**

I kicked the **ball**
right through the **wall.**

Ran up the **field**
Their fate was **sealed.**

I aimed at the **goal**
I missed the **hole.**

I stamped! I **fought**!
The balls had been **caught.**

I would not let it **rest**,
I tried to **protest**.

I got a red **card,**
after playing so **hard.**

Disqualified!
I really **tried**.

The referee was **UNFAIR**!

MESSAGE TO PLANET ZEN...

EARTH PEOPLE ARE FANATICAL ABOUT A GAME CALLED FOOTBALL.

THE PLAYERS, WHO ARE IN TWO TEAMS, USE TACTICS TO KICK A BALL INTO THEIR NET ON A FIELD. THE REFEREE IS THERE TO MAKE SURE THE GAME IS PLAYED FAIRLY, BUT IN MY CASE HE WAS UNJUST.

IT'S A GREAT GAME FOR THE ALIENS OF PLANET ZEN, SO I'VE COLLECTED SOME SPECIMENS.

I'VE COLLECTED SOME SAMPLES SPECIMENS:

- A BALL
- A FOOTBALL SHIRT
- A PICTURE OF A CELEBRITY WITH A FANCY HAIR CUT
- A RATTLE

READ	COPY	COVER & SPELL
threw		
through		
rough		
tough		
enough		
thorough		
thoroughly		
fought		
bought		
brought		
thought		

ZOGGY'S TENTH CHALLENGE

POLICE NOTICE

NO SPACE CRAFTS

Round the world in 24 hours.

When Zoggy returns to his spacecraft, he sees a **Police notice**.

He decides that it is necessary to move his spacecraft, so he starts up the engines and accelerates off.

He ascends **up, up, up, up,** and, **down, down, down...**

Zoggi says:

"words like prin**cess** and ne**cess**ary are easy to spell if you remember **cess**."

1. When **c** is followed by a **ce**, **ci** or **cy** sound, it is soft like **mice**.

2. When you have **c** followed by an **a**, it is hard like **cat**.

3. If you have two **cc**... the first sound is hard, but the second is soft like **success**.

READ	COPY	COVER & SPELL
spacecraft		
notice		
necessary		
ascend		
descend		
policeman		
succeed		
success		
accept		
accelerate		

Zoggy **might** get **frightened,** because he has landed his spacecraft **right** at the top of a **high** mountain. AH! I'd rather be under a cool fountain.

EAGLES SOAR

WOLVES HOWL.

'IGH' comes from an old English spelling.

"Help!" says Zoggy "I'm scared of

Zoggy might get frightened, because he has landed his spacecraft on a frozen iceberg.

He is *surrounded* by ice
and it is **not** very nice.

Polar bears GROWL.

Husky dogs BARK.

Snow falls.

Zoggy says, **"I am scared of being frozen."**

Zoggy might get frightened, because he has landed his spacecraft right in the middle of a hot desert.

He sees a sandstorm and prickly cactus.

Zoggy says, **"I am frightened because…"**

Zoggy might get frightened, because he has landed his spacecraft right in the middle of a safari park.

Zoggy says, "**B**ig **Ele**phants **ar**e not **u**gly. They are beautiful**."**

Zoggy says, "Is that a lion over there?"

Zoggy says, "I'm getting out of here!"

Zoggy might get frightened, because he has landed his spacecraft right in the middle of a firing range.

The soldiers move forward and fire, pretending they are at war.

Zoggy might get frightened, because he has landed his space craft right in the middle of a shopping mall.

He sees: people laughing, ladies with daughters, mothers' with babies.

Suddenly, a naughty baby catches sight of Zoggy and starts to scream. Zoggy is distraught. What a noise! She ought to be taught that aliens from Zen are not scary. Zoggy pulls a clown face and the baby's screams turn to laughter. Her mother turns round, but Zoggy has already launched his spacecraft.

ZOGGY REPORTS BACK TO ZEN...

I COULDN'T BEAR THE ICE, I CAN'T GO BACK TO THE ICEBERGS, I DON'T LIKE MOUNTAINS WHERE WOLVES HOWL AND I DON'T LIKE THE VAST SANDY DESERT. I REALLY WASN'T SCARED OF THE LION, BUT I DON'T LIKE ENTERTAINING THE BABIES AT THE SHOPPING MALL. HARD WORK!

READ	COPY	COVER & SPELL
couldn't		
can't		
doesn't		
don't		
wasn't		
didn't		
laughs		
daughter		
naughty		
taught		
caught		
distraught		
ought		
lady		
ladies		
baby		
babies		
beautiful		
pretty		
people		
howl		
growl		
scowl		

SPELLING RULE: Plurals - **'y' ends 'ies'**

READ	COPY	COVER & SPELL	SOUND
might			**GHT** is an old English Spelling
fright			
frightened			
right			
mountain			**OU**
fountain			
height			an exception to the rule 'i' before 'e' except after 'c'.
supply			
supplies			**y**' is _removed_ if you add an '**i**'.
cry			
cries			
cried			
try			
tries			
roar			
soar			
weight			
eight			
high			
height			
continuous			
fabulous			
country			
cousin			
famous			
surrounded			
grounded			
rounded			
grow			
blow			
war			
towards			
forwards			

ZOGGY'S ELEVENTH CHALLENGE

Zoggy returns from his journey round earth...

... and lands in a wood. Is he lost? Zoggy **cries**. Zoggy **cried**. He is **crying** space tears.

REPORT BACK TO ZEN...

I'M LOST IN A WOOD WITH TREES. IT'S BOILING HOT. I'M EXPLORING THE TERRAIN. EARTH PEOPLE ARE SITTING OUT ON THE GRASS ON MATS. THEY EAT FOOD FROM BASKETS.

WAIT! I KNOW THESE EARTHLINGS...

Zoggy is reunited with his earth friends.

They are having a picnic.

Dan **carries** a bottle of drink.

Grace is **carrying** the picnic basket.

Dan **carried** the mat.

Dan **tries** to be good.

Tom is **trying** to be helpful, but he drops the basket and a sausage falls on the grass.

Grace **tried** to pick up the spilt sausage, but the dog got there first.

Dan **hurries** towards the wood.

Tom **hurried** to the tree.

Grace is **hurrying** to put the mat down, so they can start eating.

Zoggy says,

"I've recorded some earthlings speech on my zamcorder to take back and show the people of Zen. Note the kinds of food that earthlings eat on picnics.

- "WHERE SHALL WE SIT?"

- "WE WERE HERE LAST YEAR. HERE IS A GOOD PLACE. NO! OVER THERE!"

- "WHO SPILT THAT DRINK?"

- "WHOSE SANDWICH IS THE DOG EATING?"

- "WHAT WOULD YOU LIKE?"

- "THOSE SAUSAGE ROLLS ARE GOOD."

- "I DON'T LIKE PEPPERONI PIZZA. YUK!"

- "I WANT ANOTHER COOKIE."

- "I CAN'T MANAGE ANY MORE OF THOSE SCOTCH EGGS."

- "WHEN ARE WE GOING HOME?"

READ	COPY	COVER & SPELL
where		
were		
while		
smile		
here		
there		
their		
who		
whose		
whole		
these		
those		
people		
answer		
when		
what		
want		
went		
can't		
didn't		
cry		
cried		
crying		
hurry		
hurries		
hurried		
try		
tries		
trying		
carry		
carrying		
carries		
carried		

"**Let's picnic guys**," says Zoggy. "I've decided we should try this experience on Zen!"

I am sitting on the edge
Of the grass, by the hedge.

I am eating so much food,
I'm in a splendid mood.

I've had coleslaw made of cabbage,
Which is more than I can manage,

Sausage rolls and salad leaves,
Crunchy crisps, if you please.

Lots of ham,
A sponge with jam.

Some ginger beer,
Too fizzy, I fear.

Earth food is nourishing;
The people encouraging.

I'm just glad I'm accepted:
I haven't been rejected.

I may be a stranger,
I present no danger.

Although I'm a spy,
I'm a decent guy.

Got the right image,
To be part of the village.

READ	COPY	COVER & SPELL
greedy		
eating		
coleslaw		
cabbage		
manager		
sponge		
ginger		
stranger		
danger		
village		
imagine		
guy		
decent		
experience		
accepted		
rejected		
nourish		
country		
encourage		

Zoggy says, "When 'g' has 'ge', 'gi' and 'gy' it makes a *__soft sound__* like 'j' but 'g' followed by 'gu' is *__hard__*. For example, '*guy*.'

ZOGGY'S FINAL CHALLENGE

"How are you Zoggy?"

"I'm good, but my mission is nearly over and I must finish writing this report."

Help Zoggy write his report:

DATE:	PLANET EARTH
PEOPLE	
APPEARANCE	
CHARACTER	
FOOD	
CLOTHES	
ACTIVITIES	
ACHIEVEMENTS	

Can you think of any more?

Zoggy painted some pictures of his adventures on planet Earth. He will take them back to Zen, which is three million light years away in deep space.

Help Zoggy fill in his sketchbook.

Does Zoggy have answers to **all** his questions?

Can you help Zoggy fill in his questionnaire and learn these tricky words?

Zoggy says, "Can you spell all the <u>underlined</u> words?"

```
ABOUT PEOPLE:

Why do humans laugh?
           yawn?
           cough?

Why do they have hands not claws or paws?

Why do people work all the time?

Why is money so important?

Why do they listen to music?

Why do they spread margarine on their bread?

Why do earth kids go to school and get an education?

Why do they have to remember facts for examinations?

Why do they read newspapers to get information?

Why do kids wear uniforms at school?

Why do earth people have conversations?

Why do earth people have furniture in their homes?

Why do earth people get prescriptions?

Why do earth people have associations and organisations?

Why do earth people speak on mobile phones?
```

Why do earth people take **photographs** on **digital** cameras?

Why do they **quarrel** and **squabble**?

Why don't humans travel the **universe**?

And what is the **population** of earth?

Do you know?

ABOUT CREATURES ON EARTH:

Why do horses **neigh** and dogs bark?

Why do they have **swarms** of horrible stingy **wasps**?

Why do pigs eat from a **trough**?

Why are there strange **animals** in the **jungle** like **elephants**, **giraffes** and monkeys?

Why do **dolphins** swim in the sea?

Why do **gnats** fly?
     rats **gnaw**?
     and **gnomes** sit on lawns?

Do humans really believe in the existence of **ghosts**?
                                     haunted houses?
                                     aliens?
                                   flying **saucers**?

Why is the weather always **humid** and wet and never **warm**?

ABOUT ME:

Will I be able to launch my zennel spacecraft without **causing** a **media sensation**?

Why are the people of Zen so small?
                            so different?
                            so **superior**?

Why are earthlings so **inferior**?

Why do we eat **worms**?

READ	COPY	COVER & SPELL
laugh		
yawn		
cough		
claw		
work		
money		
listen		
music		
margarine		
school		
education		
examination		
information		
conversation		
population		
prescription		
association		
organisation		
uniform		
universe		
newspaper		
mobile phone		
photograph		
digital		
quarrel		
squabble		
swarm		
wasp		
warm		
animal		
jungle		
trough		
haunted		
saucer		
superior, believe		
inferior		

THE BEST THINGS ABOUT EARTH:

THE WORST THINGS ABOUT EARTH:

SPOT THE SILENT LETTERS

READ	COPY	COVER & SPELL
dolphin		
gnat		
gnaw		
gnome		
knife		
knight		
thumb		
comb		
knew		
know		
knowing		
solemn		
lamb		
autumn		

Before he returns to Zen, Zoggy photographs his new friends with his digital camera and writes some notes.

He regrets having to leave earth. He remembers his adventures and refuses to forget. He realises he must go back.

*Some words have **prefixes** like '**re**' or '**de**'*

THE .... FAMILY

MR/MISTER	MRS/MISTRESS
	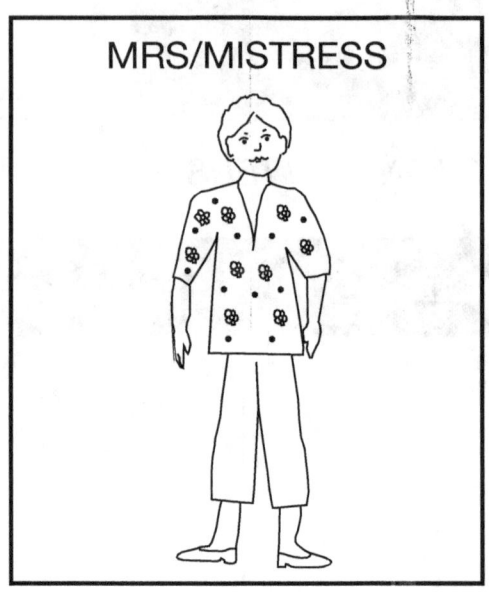

DAN	TOM	GRACE

Used to be naughty, but now is usually good.	A clever, generous boy, who is a genius.	Is always curious and inspected my spacecraft.

What are Zen children like Zoggy?
Do they obey their parents or do they disobey them?

READ	COPY	COVER & SPELL
listen		
human		
people		
answer		
question		
questionnaire		
Mr		
Mrs		
myself		
themselves		
boring		
snoring		
photograph		
digital camera		

ZOGGI wipes away a tear
and waves goodbye.

> I regret
> leaving earth.
> My break
> Has been refreshing.
> My report will remind me,
> I have so much to remember.
> I've realised I am lucky...
>
>
> ...I must not delay.

READ	COPY	COVER & SPELL
picture		
adventure		
future		
beautiful		
forward		
war		
towards		
fire		
firing		
tire		
tiring		
smile		
smiling		
pretty		
country		
cousin		
famous		
nourish		

SPELLING RULE: Drop **'e' if you add an 'i'**

www.ingramcontent.com/pod-product-compliance
Lightning Source LLC
Chambersburg PA
CBHW080128110526
44587CB00019BA/3397